MYSTERY HISTORY OF A
PHARAOH'S TOMB

JIM PIPE

Illustrated by Mike Bell, Mike Lacey, and Roger Hutchins

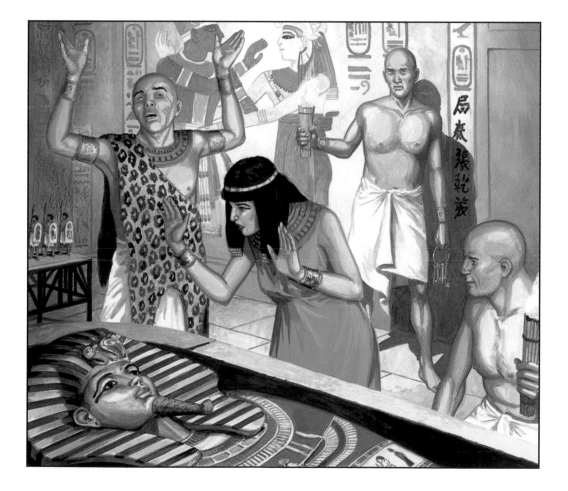

COPPER BEECH BOOKS
BROOKFIELD, CONNECTICUT

© Aladdin Books Ltd 1997

Designed and produced by
Aladdin Books Ltd
28 Percy Street
London W1P 0LD

First published in
the United States in 1997 by
Copper Beech Books,
an imprint of
The Millbrook Press
2 Old New Milford Road
Brookfield, CT 06804

Consultant
Dr. Anne Millard
Editor
Jon Richards
Designed by
David West Children's Books
Designer
Simon Morse
Illustrated by
Mike Bell – Specs Art
Mike Lacey
Roger Hutchins

Additional illustrations by
David Burroughs
Rob Shone

Printed in Belgium
All rights reserved

Library of Congress
Cataloging-in-Publication Data
Pipe, Jim, 1966-
Pharaoh's tomb / by Jim Pipe ;
illustrated by Mike Bell ... [et al.].
p. cm. — (Mystery history of a—)
Includes index.
Summary: Uses mazes, puzzles, and
games to provide a look at various
aspects of life in an ancient Egyptian
city.
ISBN 0-7613-0591-2 (Trade HC). –
– ISBN 0-7613-0600-5 (S&L HC)
1. Cities and towns, Ancient–
–Egypt—Juvenile literature.
2. Egypt—Civilization—To 332 B.C.-
–Juvenile literature. [1.Egypt–
–Civilization—To 332 B.C.] I. Bell,
Mike, ill. II. Title. III. Series:
Mystery history.
DT61.P64 1997   96-50172
932—dc21   CIP AC

Contents

THE PHARAOH'S TOMB

For 3,000 years, the kings of ancient Egypt battled to outwit the thieves who robbed their graves. This was a serious business, for the Egyptians believed that the future prosperity of their country depended on the pharaoh. If his body was protected by the tomb, then two of his spirits – the *ka* and the *ba* (see page 25) – could live there forever and Egypt would be blessed by the gods. The very first tombs were only holes in the ground (*right*). In about 2600 B.C., King Zoser built the first pyramid with platforms placed above each other (*left*). This led to the great, straight-sided pyramids at Giza (about 2500 B.C.).
To the pharaoh of our story (who lived in the New Kingdom, 1550–1070 B.C. – *see page 5*) these massive buildings were useless, because they showed grave robbers exactly where kings were buried. So later pharaohs built underground tombs that were heavily guarded.

THE MYSTERY OF HISTORY

We know a lot about the ancient Egyptians from tombs and temples. But there's still so much we don't know. So as you read, try to imagine the sights, the sounds, and the smells. Who knows, your picture of Egyptian life might be right. That's the real mystery of history!

USING MYSTERY HISTORY

You'll find that *Mystery History of a Pharaoh's Tomb* is packed with puzzles and mysteries for you to solve. But before you go any further, read the instructions below to get the most out of the book!

Hunt the Assassin

One of the pharaoh's courtiers is out to kill him! No one knows who, but on page 29 some likely suspects have been lined up. To help you figure out which one of them is the assassin, clues are given in six Hunt the Assassin boxes. For example, if you think that b is the right answer to the question, then it might tell you that the assassin is wearing a wig. To get the right clues, however, you need the right answer – and that means reading the book carefully! Happy hunting!

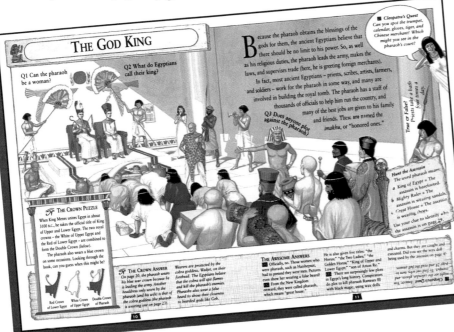

Cleopatra's Quest

Try to find the objects that are cleverly hidden in the artwork, then guess if you would really find them in ancient Egypt!

History Mysteries

Dotted around the page are questions like: Q1 What is the worst job in ancient Egypt? Think about these questions before reading the answer in The Awesome Answers.

Pharaoh's Puzzles

This sign indicates a special puzzle that is anything from a maze to a mystery word written in hieroglyphs. Answers are given in The Awesome Answers.

True or False

Some pages have a teasing True or False question with an answer (on page 29) that may surprise you!

The Awesome Answers

Answers to Cleopatra's Quest, the History Mysteries, and the Pharaoh's Puzzles are given in this panel at the bottom of each page.

Tomb Robbers' Game

At the back of the book (page 28–29) are full answers to Cleopatra's Quest and True or False, a lineup of suspects (one of whom has tried to poison the pharaoh), and, last but not least, a fantastic cutaway of a tomb that is also an exciting puzzle game (right!)

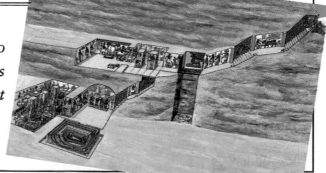

THE MIGHTY NILE

Q1 How important are canals to Egypt?

FLOOD PUZZLE

From the height of the flood waters, the Egyptians can guess how their crops will grow. The height is measured in cubits (about 20 inches). A visitor to Egypt, writing in about A.D. 50, says that:

▲ A rise of only 13 cubits brings starvation

▲ A rise of 15 cubits brings suffering

▲ A rise of 17 cubits brings security

What do you think a rise of 20 cubits brings? How high is this in feet?

Mediterranean Sea

Giza
Memphis
LOWER EGYPT
Red Sea
Nile River
UPPER EGYPT
Thebes
Flood area

FLOOD PUZZLE ANSWER

A rise of 20 cubits brings disaster, because it washes away the mud brick houses. However, as the Egyptians build their homes on the remains of older buildings, the villages rise above the fields over many years. During a flood, these villages form small islands (see main picture). A flood of 20 cubits is about 33 feet.

Q2 How ancient is ancient Egypt?

⊡ **Cleopatra's Quest**
Can you spot the canoe, water skier, pillow, wig, and fishing net in the main picture? Which might you expect to see in ancient Egypt?

True or False?
The pyramids are built by slaves.

The ancient Egyptians live on a strip of land on either side of the long Nile River (*see map on page 4*). Once a year, the river floods, and for four months covers the Nile valley. It leaves behind a layer of black mud that nourishes the farmers' crops for the rest of the year. Because of this black mud, the ancient Egyptians call their land *Kemit*, or the "Black Land."

The flood seems like a magical event to the Egyptians, since their country is surrounded by the "Red Land," or desert, on all sides, and has little rain. It is also a symbol of their pharaoh's (king's) power. To the Egyptians, only the pharaoh can satisfy the gods and bring the life-giving waters of the flood, because he is the son of the sun god Re.

THE AWESOME ANSWERS

Q1 They're vital! By about 3500 B.C., North Africa is turning into desert. Only the Nile doesn't dry up, so the Egyptians dig canals to water their crops throughout the year. Even pictures of Menes, the first pharaoh, show him digging a canal (3100 B.C.).

Q2 Very. The pyramids have stood for 2,500 years when the Romans take over in 30 B.C.! Egyptian history is split into the Archaic period (3100–2575 B.C.), the Old Kingdom (2040–1640 B.C.), the Middle Kingdom (2040–1640 B.C.), and the New Kingdom (1550–1070 B.C.). In these periods, the pharaoh rules supreme. In between are times of civil war or invasion. From 1070 B.C., Egypt is ruled by a succession of foreign rulers.

⊡ *Cleopatra's Quest Answer: You might see all of them except the water-skier. To find out why, turn to page 28.*

5

THE GREAT TEMPLE

I n such a magical land, it's not surprising that ancient Egyptians are very religious. Each night, when the sun god Re disappears in the west, they believe that he is traveling across the sky in a boat. As Re's son, the pharaoh must ensure that Re will appear the next morning by making daily offerings to him. He also prays to other gods in the temple. In return, the gods make the temple their home and show favor to the pharaoh and his people. Because of these powers, Egyptians have a special respect for their pharaoh, who is much more than just a king. He is their link to the gods – their savior.

Q1 Why is the temple so huge?

📷 *Cleopatra's Quest*
Can you spot the sundial, slot machine, crocodile, sniffer dogs, bell, and scaffolding? Which might you see in an ancient Egyptian temple?

📷 *Cleopatra's Quest Answer:*
At different times in Egypt's history, you might see all of them apart from the bell! To find out why, *turn to page 28.*

THE AWESOME ANSWERS

Q1 When a city is chosen as the pharaoh's capital, its local god becomes famous – and its temple grows richer and larger. Every town has a temple dedicated to its god or family of gods. Not all temples are huge, but all are built to the same plan. The sanctuary (where offerings of food are given to the gods) is reached via courtyards and halls with many columns. The lower part of every temple represents the earth, out of which grow columns shaped like lotus plants or palms. The ceiling represents heaven, and is painted with stars and birds.

Q2 Where does everyone pray?

Hunt the Assassin
The ancient Egyptian name for Egypt, Kemit, *means*:

a Mighty River = The assassin is bald.

b Black Land = The assassin is wearing a wig.

c Red Land = The assassin is wearing a headdress or helmet.

Use your clue to identify who the assassin is on page 29.

True or False?
Pharaohs have lots of money.

Q3 What is going on?

👁 MAGIC PUZZLE

The lofty gods of the temples play a major part in daily life. However, most Egyptians also use a little magic to solve their everyday problems. When they pray to local gods (can you spot a small shrine on page 16?), they sometimes carve ears (*left*) next to the prayer so that the god may hear them better.

Magic is used to ease problems like disease or natural perils. Magical charms are often worn on necklaces and bracelets. Spells are sometimes written on them. What do you think this charm (*right*) is supposed to protect you against?

Q2 They don't! Egyptian temples are homes for the gods, not places for everyone to pray. Only priests, priestesses, and royalty may enter the temple. Most Egyptians pray at home to gods and goddesses like Taueret, a gentle hippopotamus who helps women in childbirth.

Q3 The chief priest is leading a procession into the temple. This is a solemn affair, quite unlike the popular processions that take place in the towns. At the festival of Bes, dancers lead the way wearing bright masks, while the townspeople follow or cheer from the rooftops.

👁 MAGIC PUZZLE ANSWER
This is a magical carving, called a stela, that protects against natural dangers. Here the god Harpocrates is standing on two crocodiles, stopping them from grabbing any members of the family, and holding two snakes to prevent them from biting anyone.

LAND OF THE GODS

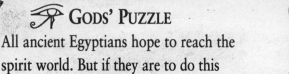

𓂀 GODS' PUZZLE

All ancient Egyptians hope to reach the spirit world. But if they are to do this successfully, they must keep the gods on their side – and there are a lot of gods and goddesses to please!

Each god and goddess controls an aspect of life or death and must be respected. Together they control the world and everything that happens in it.

The Egyptians want to be close to their gods and goddesses, but no human is allowed to look like them.

However, hidden among the twelve gods shown here are three that are not Egyptian. Which three are they, and what religion do they come from?

Q1 Who is the most powerful god or goddess?

Amon-Re
The sun god

Osiris
God of the Underworld

Bastet
Cat goddess of joy

Sobek
Crocodile-headed god of water

Nut
Goddess of the sky

Thor
God of thunder

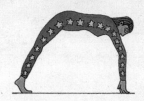

Thoth
Ibis-headed god of wisdom and writing

Athena
Goddess of wisdom

Anubis
Jackal-headed guardian of the dead

Khnum
Ram-headed potter god

Isis
Goddess of women and children

Kali
Goddess of destruction

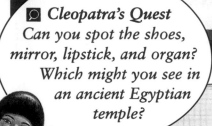

○ *Cleopatra's Quest*
Can you spot the shoes, mirror, lipstick, and organ? Which might you see in an ancient Egyptian temple?

○ *Cleopatra's Quest Answer:*
You might see the shoes, mirror, and lipstick, but not the organ. To find out why, turn to page 28 and read the full answer.

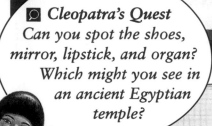

𓂀 GODS' PUZZLE ANSWER

The three who don't belong in ancient Egypt are Thor (Viking), Athena (ancient Greek), and Kali (Hindu). However, in the ancient world, most religions worship gods from older civilizations: e.g., the ancient Romans worship the Egyptian goddess Isis. Even our seven days of the week are named after the Roman, Saxon, and Viking gods. Wednesday is named after Saxon god Woden in English, and Roman god Mercury in French (Mercredi). The length of our year is based on the Egyptian calendar. It also has 365 days.

The pharaoh relies on the priests to help him carry out his duties. Here, they are helping him in his offerings to the gods. But their most important task is to help the pharaoh's soul reach the spirit world when he dies. If the pharaoh's spirit lives forever, then the Egyptians believe they will have the blessing of the gods – and everlasting prosperity. So even in life, the pharaoh prepares for death. He must build a tomb that will protect his body for eternity.

Q2 What are the priests doing?

THE AWESOME ANSWERS

Q1 Isis, the loving mother goddess is believed to have the most magic power. But Amon-Re is responsible for all living things. He takes many forms, such as Khepri, the scarab god, Re-Harakhty, the great hawk in the sky, and Amun-Re, the "hidden" god.

Q2 Here, in the inner sanctuary, the high priest (wearing a leopard skin) opens the shrine with the words, "I am the pure one," to reveal the dazzling golden statue of the god Aton-Re. With him are the pharaoh, and priests carrying incense burners, standards, and lamps. A priest is scattering holy water from the temple's sacred lake over the floor.

Others are carrying loaves of bread and vases of wine or beer to feed the god, and one carries a broom for sweeping the floor after the ceremony is over, to remove all trace of human presence from this holy place.

THE GOD KING

Q1 Can the pharaoh be a woman?

Q2 What do Egyptians call their king?

𓂀 THE CROWN PUZZLE

When King Menes unites Egypt in about 3100 B.C., he takes the official title of King of Upper and Lower Egypt. The two royal crowns – the White of Upper Egypt and the Red of Lower Egypt – are combined to form the Double Crown (*below*).

The pharaoh also wears a blue crown on some occasions. Looking through the book, can you guess when this might be?

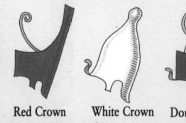

Red Crown of Lower Egypt   White Crown of Upper Egypt   Double Crown of Pharaoh

𓂀 THE CROWN ANSWER

On page 20, the pharaoh wears his blue war crown because he is leading the army. Another headdress only worn by the pharaoh (and his wife) is that of the cobra goddess (the pharaoh is wearing one on page 23). *Wearers are protected by the cobra goddess, Wadjet, on their forehead. The Egyptians believe that the cobra will spit flames and kill the pharaoh's enemies. Pharaohs also wear a false beard to show their closeness to bearded gods like Geb.*

Because the pharaoh obtains the blessings of the gods for them, the ancient Egyptians believe that there should be no limit to his power. So, as well as his religious duties, the pharaoh leads the army, makes the laws, and supervises trade (here, he is greeting foreign merchants).

In fact, most ancient Egyptians – priests, scribes, artists, farmers, and soldiers – work for the pharaoh in some way, and many are involved in building the royal tomb. The pharaoh has a staff of thousands of officials to help him run the country, and many of the best jobs are given to his family and friends. These are named the *imakhu*, or "honored ones."

Q3 Does anyone plot against the pharaoh?

Cleopatra's Quest
Can you spot the trumpet, calendar, gloves, tiger, and Chinese merchant? Which might you see in the pharaoh's court?

True or False? Priests take a bath four times a day.

Hunt the Assassin
The word pharaoh means:

a *King of Egypt* = The assassin is barefooted.

b *Mighty Ruler* = The assassin is wearing sandals.

c *Great House* = The assassin is wearing shoes.

Use your clue to identify who the assassin is on page 29.

THE AWESOME ANSWERS

Q1 Officially, no. Those women who were pharaoh, such as Hatshepsut, had to pretend they were men. Pictures even show her wearing a false beard!

Q2 From the New Kingdom onward, they were called pharaoh, which means "great house."

He is also given five titles: "the Horus;" "the Two Ladies;" "the Golden Horus;" "King of Upper and Lower Egypt;" "son of Amon Re."

Q3 There are surprisingly few plots in Egypt's long history. Conspirators do plot to kill pharaoh Rameses III with black magic, using wax dolls

and charms. But they are caught and executed. Did you see the wax doll being used by the assassin on page 4?

Cleopatra's Quest Answer: You might see the calendar, gloves, and trumpet. To find out why, turn to page 28 and read the full answer.

THE KING'S OFFICIALS

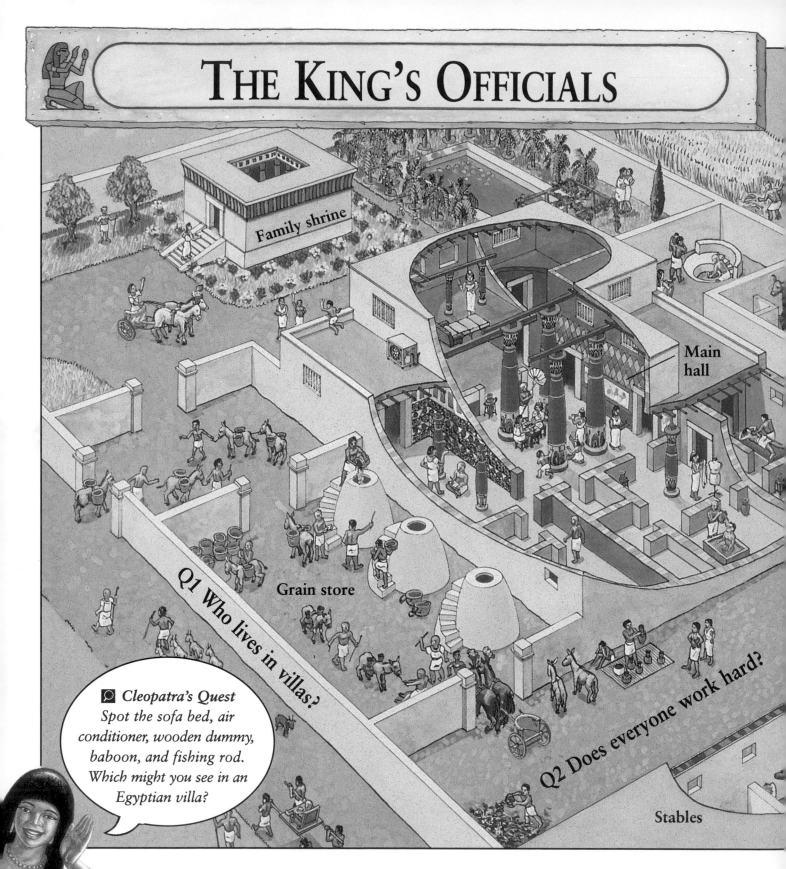

Family shrine

Main hall

Q1 Who lives in villas?

Grain store

Q2 Does everyone work hard?

Stables

Cleopatra's Quest
Spot the sofa bed, air conditioner, wooden dummy, baboon, and fishing rod. Which might you see in an Egyptian villa?

THE AWESOME ANSWERS

Q1 Only wealthy families – most Egyptians live in simple houses. But all buildings are cool. Walls are coated in limestone plaster to reflect the sun's heat, and windows are placed high in the walls to catch cool breezes from the north.

Q2 Most Egyptians, including rich people, many of whom are top officials, work for nine days and have the tenth day off. To avoid the midday heat, craftsmen labor for four hours in the morning, break for a meal, and then work another shift in the late afternoon. But not everyone is so hardworking: A letter written in 1500 B.C. by the Mayor of Thebes criticizes a farmer for being lazy – and for eating in bed!

Cleopatra's Quest Answer: You may see the baboon and the fishing rod! *To find out why, turn to page 28.*

The pharaoh's chief official is the vizier, who oversees everything. Other important officials are the Chief of Canals and the Master of Works. But Egypt is such a big country that it is impossible for court officials to be everywhere, so local districts are run by governors. Though they often live in grand villas (like the one here), their power is limited.

Apart from the pharaoh, the high priests are the most powerful people. Their power comes from large areas of land given to their temples by prvious pharaohs to ensure a proper burial. However, as the pharaoh appoints who becomes high priest, he still has control over them.

Hunt the Assassin
Goddess Bastet looks like:

a A *cat* = The assassin is wearing a long white robe.

b A *ram* = The assassin is wearing a short white skirt.

c A *falcon* = The assassin is wearing a short blue skirt.

Use your clue to identify the assassin on page 29.

Kitchens

Noble's bedroom

Servants' quarters

Q3 Why is washing clothes so dangerous?

CLOTHES PUZZLE

Egyptian clothes are made of linen woven from flax (a type of plant). Poorer people wear loincloths of coarse fabric; the pharaoh and his courtiers wear the finest linen. Fine clothes have many pleats, but such fancy garments are not ideal for everyone. Who might wear leather padding on their skirts (*top*) or a net of beads over their clothes (*left*)?

Q3 Because crocodiles often attack laundry workers as they work in the shallow waters at the edge of the river. Washing other people's clothes in cleanliness-mad ancient Egypt also means that everyone else looks down at you!

CLOTHES ANSWER
Sailors wear leather pads on campaign to stop the backs of their skirts from wearing away while rowing. Rich people wear the nets of colorful beads over their clothes to show off their wealth.

SCRIBBLING SCRIBES

The pharaoh relies on an army of scribes to keep detailed records of what is happening in his kingdom. These record-keepers and letter-writers are highly valued, as most Egyptians cannot read the complicated symbols written on temples and tombs.

In return for their special skills, the scribes are given authority and freedom from taxes. Some are even given the chance to achieve everlasting fame through the words they write on the walls of the pharaoh's tomb.

Hieroglyphs

Q1 How do you become a scribe?

Q2 What are they writing?

Hieratic script

Q3 How can we read the symbols?

THE AWESOME ANSWERS

Q1 Some scribes begin their education at four (the youngest boys wear their hair in a pigtail at the side of the head). The training is hard and lasts for about five years.

Q2 A form of picture writing called hieroglyphs. It is deliberately complicated so that few people can understand it – and the scribes can keep their special position in society. Hieroglyphs are carved on walls and stone tablets, and written on papyrus. Papyrus is a type of paper made from reeds that are soaked, hammered flat, and then dried into sheets. For business letters the scribes use a form of writing called hieratic, which they can write much faster than hieroglyphs. From about 800 B.C. onward, an even faster form of writing is used, called demotic.

👁 HIEROGLYPH PUZZLE

The word hieroglyph is ancient Greek for "sacred carvings." Hieroglyphs are written in many different ways: from left to right, from right to left, or from top to bottom. If an animal faces right in a set of hieroglyphs, you read it from right to left. If it faces left, you read it from left to right. There are two main types of hieroglyphs. The first are like single letters (*below*):

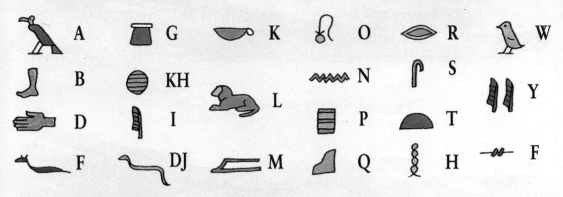

A   G   K   O   R   W
B   KH   N   S
D   I   L   P   T   Y
F   DJ   M   Q   H   F

a

b

c

The names of Egyptian kings and queens appear within an oval frames called cartouches. The scholar Champollion (*see below*) figured out the hieroglyphics using cartouches of names like Cleopatra, Pepy, and Ptolemy.

Using the alphabet above, can you match **a**, **b**, and **c** to these three names? Then try to write your own name in hieroglyphics.

However, many hieroglyphs are more like Chinese characters – they stand for whole words as well as letters. Can you match these hieroglyphs to the words below them?

1   2   3   4   5   6   7   8   9   10
11   12   13   14   15   16   17

Duck, Board game, Wing, Sun, Head, Baboon, Ram, Palace wall, Cat, Bee, Nest, Nurse, Pharaoh, Stairway, Star, Crocodile, Ear.

> **◎ Cleopatra's Quest**
> Can you spot the typewriter, quill pen, inkwell, and ruler? Which might you see in an ancient Egyptian classroom?

Q3 When the last Egyptian temple closes in the 6th century A.D., the skill of reading hieroglyphs is lost. But in 1822, Frenchman Jean-François Champollion figures out the symbols using the Rosetta Stone. This contains writing in Greek, demotic, and hieroglyphs. By comparing names in Greek with hieroglyphs, he slowly translates the Egyptian text.

𓅿 HIEROGLYPH ANSWER

a Ptolemy, *b* Cleopatra, *c* Pepy. 1 Bee, 2 Stairway, 3 Board game, 4 Wing, 5 Sun, 6 Head, 7 Ear, 8 Baboon, 9 Palace Wall, 10 Cat, 11 Duck, 12 Nest, 13 Nurse, 14 Pharaoh, 15 Ram, 16 Star, 17

Cleopatra's Quest Answer: You'd only see a type of inkwell! To find out why, turn to page 28.

OUT IN THE FIELDS

Q1 How is the wheat harvested?

Hippopotamus hunt

Reaping

Ninety percent of Egyptians are farmers who never enter the great temples or the court. However, their lives are still closely linked to the pharaoh. For farming is the source of the pharaoh's great wealth, and every year scribes figure out the tax that all farmers pay to the king. If they don't pay up, they are beaten.

During the flood, farmers help with public works, such as dragging stone blocks on sleds to the site of a new temple or tomb. They also repair any damage to the canals. Many do this willingly, because they hope the pharaoh will look after them in the spirit world in return for their labor.

THE AWESOME ANSWERS

Q1 After the wheat is cut (reaped), donkeys are used to carry it to the threshing floor. Cattle are driven across the wheat to separate the grain from the husk (threshing). The wheat is tossed into the air, the lighter husk is allowed to blow away (winnowing), and the grain is put into baskets for storage. Though Egypt is a very fertile land, there are bad harvests, so the grain is stored in large granaries until it is needed. Wheat is ground into flour and used to make bread. The Egyptians also grow barley for beer, flax for clothes, and many vegetables.

Q2 Yes. They raise cattle, sheep, pigs, ducks, geese, and goats, and some keep bees for honey, which is used for sweetening. An important measure of a person's wealth is the number of cattle they own. Like harvested crops, each year livestock is counted and taxed for the pharaoh.

Q2 Do the Egyptians keep animals?

Cleopatra's Quest
Can you spot the boomerang, scythe, and underwear? Which don't belong in the ancient Egyptian countryside?

Bird Hunt

Shaduf (used for lifting water)

Winnowing

Threshing

Q3 Which animals do the Egyptians hunt?

EGYPTIAN MATH PUZZLE

The Egyptians are great mathematicians – but math is a closely guarded secret (perhaps to make tax collecting easier). Egyptian numbers are made up of symbols (*below*):

= 1	= 1,000	= 100,000
= 10		
= 100	= 10,000	= 1,000,000

These symbols are then used to build up larger numbers:

7 =   IIIIIII   36 = ∩∩∩ IIIIII   422 = 𝓎𝓎𝓎𝓎 ∩∩ II

But math isn't easy for the tax-collecting scribe. Convert the following two numbers into Egyptian symbols – 62,351 and 29,716 – then see how easy it is to add them. Check your answer by using modern numerals.

Q3 Fish are caught with small nets or with hooks or spears. Birds are usually caught with clever spring-loaded nets. Hippos are a danger to rafts and boats, so they are also hunted. Pharaoh Tuthmosis III boasted that he killed 120 elephants and 120 lions in a single hour of hunting!

EGYPTIAN MATH ANSWER
The answer in ancient Egyptian is:

or 92,067 in Arabic numerals.

Cleopatra's Quest Answer:
Amazingly, you might see all of these things except the scythe! To find out why, turn to page 28 to read the full answer.

THE TOMB BUILDERS

True or False?
The mummy of Rameses the Great has pepper stuffed up its nose.

Q1 What are these craftsmen making?

Q2 Do they all work on the tomb at the same time?

Hunt the Assassin
Which pharaoh built the first pyramid?

a King Menes = The assassin is wearing earrings.

b King Zoser = The assassin is wearing bracelets.

c Queen Hatshepsut = The assassin is wearing neither.

THE AWESOME ANSWERS

Q1 Everything that the pharaoh's spirit will need in the afterlife – in other words, everything he uses in day-to-day life. Most Egyptian craftsmen specialize in one skill. There are carpenters, furniture-makers, jewelers, plasterers, stone masons, sculptors, painters, potters, weavers, and glass makers.

Q2 The tomb builders are split into the left and right gangs, to work on different sides of the tomb at the same time. They live in huts above the Valley of the Kings and every eight days return home for two days of rest.

Cleopatra's Quest Answer: You might see the bag lunch, pigeon post, and spirit level! To find out why, turn to page 28 to read the full answer.

18

Most craftsmen in ancient Egypt are employed by the pharaoh or the temples. They work in large, highly organized workshops or in special gangs, like the tomb builders who live near the Valley of the Kings at Thebes. These people usually toil away in hot workshops, but here they are working near the tomb entrance. Their work is of the highest quality, to help the spirit of the pharaoh enjoy the afterlife. Each and every object built for the pharaoh's tomb must be perfect, and must last forever!

The pharaoh builds his tomb long before he expects to die, for it takes many years to finish. In theory, he finds the perfect site himself, but in practice it is usually done by his officials.

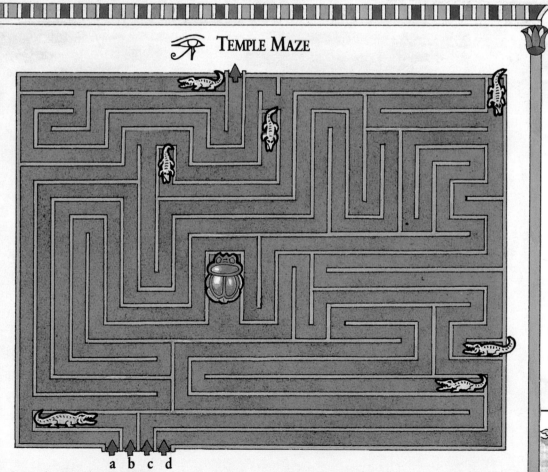

👁 TEMPLE MAZE

a b c d

According to the Greek historian Herodotus, the most remarkable tomb built by Egyptian craftsmen is the labyrinth at Lake Moeris. The building has 3,000 rooms, linked by a maze of passages. But the gigantic tomb also houses sacred crocodiles! Imagine you are a priest sent to find a sacred scarab for a ceremony. Can you work out which of routes a, b, c, or d will steer you through the labyrinth, past the scarab but away from hungry crocodiles?

MAZE ANSWER
The safe way through the labyrinth is route d!

👁 Cleopatra's Quest
Can you spot the dynamite, pneumatic drill, bag lunch, pigeon post, a level, and knitting needles? Which might you see on an Egyptian building site?

THE PHARAOH'S SOLDIERS

Q1 What weapons do Egyptian soldiers fight with?

True or False? Egyptians like their portraits painted with extra-large stomachs.

THE AWESOME ANSWERS

Q1 Egyptian soldiers use bronze axes, spears, swords, and daggers. Infantrymen carry wooden shields, which are covered in cowhide. Some men wear light body armor, but most are unprotected. The most important long-range weapon is the bow.

Chariots are used from the New Kingdom onward. They are platforms for bowmen and spear throwers.

Q2 Sometimes, tens of thousands. On his campaign through Qadesh in Syria in 1270 B.C., Rameses II has an army of about 20,000 as well as camp followers. For many centuries, armies are only formed when they are needed. But in the New Kingdom, a permanent army is formed with special generals.

Cleopatra's Quest Answer: You might see the lion, medal, and first aid kit! To find out why, turn to page 29.

○ **Cleopatra's Quest**
*Can you spot the cavalry,
elephant, medal, crossbow,
and first-aid kit? Which
wouldn't you see on
an Egyptian
battlefield?*

L ike the tomb builders, Egyptian soldiers work for the pharaoh, who is their commander-in-chief. Though Egypt is rarely threatened by invading armies, the pharaoh carries out military campaigns in Palestine and Syria, to the north, and Nubia, to the south. In peacetime, soldiers help to transport stone from the desert for public buildings.

The Egyptian army is very well organized, from the pharaoh down to officers in charge of groups of 50 soldiers. Army scribes write messages and records of the campaigns. Most soldiers fight on foot, but the Egyptians also use chariots, each manned by two soldiers and pulled by two horses. Though in tomb paintings the pharaoh is shown riding a chariot alone, in real life he has a charioteer to drive for him.

Q2 How many soldiers does the pharaoh command?

👁 MEDICINE PUZZLE

The Egyptians are very skilled at treating battlefield wounds, but their medicine is a strange mixture of good science and magic. Some cures are quite advanced, while others are ludicrous – a cure for blindness involves mashing up a pig's eye with honey and red ocher, then putting it in the patient's ear! Can you guess which of the items in this panel are used by Egyptian doctors?

magic amulet

moldy bread

needle & thread

syringe

prescription bottle

bandage

plaster cast

👁 MEDICINE ANSWER

Moldy bread is used to stop wounds from getting infected. The mold works like penicillin as a form of antibiotic! Though ancient Egyptian doctors have a huge range of surgical instruments, such as needles and scalpels, they don't have syringes (this one belongs to a Roman eye surgeon from the 2nd century A.D.). They do use bandages and splints for broken bones, but not plaster. Cures are often provided in bottles with the prescription written on them. Finally, despite their medical skill, doctors still use amulets to ward off the evil spirits. They believe these are the real cause of disease!

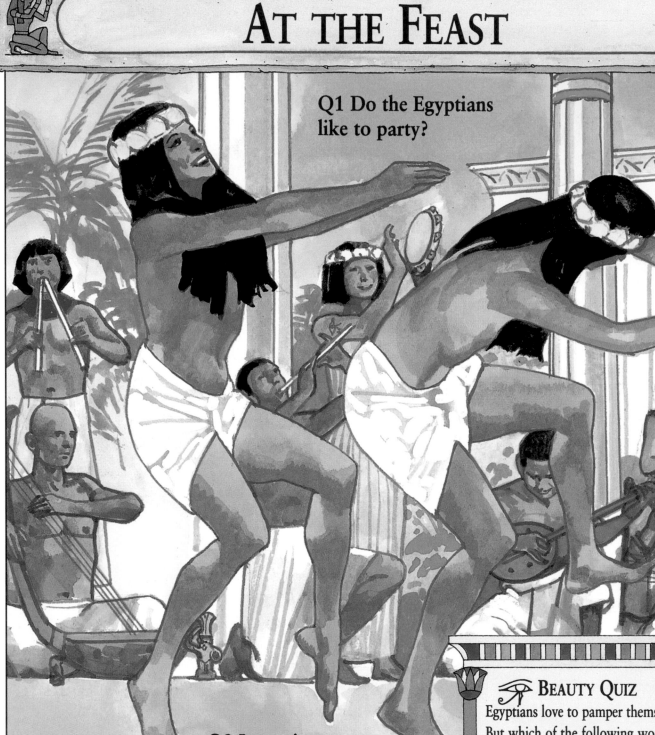

Q1 Do the Egyptians like to party?

Q2 Is music just for pleasure?

👁 BEAUTY QUIZ
Egyptians love to pamper themselves. But which of the following would they do to look beautiful?
▲ Bathe often;
▲ Have lots of massages;
▲ Wear suntan lotion;
▲ Pluck their eyebrows;
▲ If they are male, grow lovely bushy beards;
▲ Use red henna to color the palms of their hands and feet;
▲ Use eye paint made from soot.

👁 BEAUTY QUIZ ANSWER
Rich Egyptians love to bathe. They also have servants trained in the art of massage. They use suntan lotion made from oils and herbs, to protect them against the fierce sun. As for cosmetics, they color their hands and feet with henna, and use black eye paint, lipsticks, and red blush – and yes, the black is made from soot! However, the Egyptians hate body hair, so eyebrows are often plucked, and men have only small, thin beards.

Cleopatra's Quest
Can you spot the darts, mechanical toy, tattoo, board game, and drinking straw? Which might you see at the pharaoh's palace?

Y**ou** might imagine that with all his duties, which include making the sun rise every day, the pharaoh doesn't get much chance to enjoy himself. Far from it! After his official business is over each day, the pharaoh goes out hunting, or relaxes in the beautiful palace gardens.

Even after important public ceremonies, he enjoys celebratory banquets. Dancers, clowns, and musicians entertain him while servants bring dishes piled high with meat, cakes, and fruit. There is also beer and wine to drink.

True or False?
Some tombs are built with toilets.

Hunt the Assassin
What is papyrus?

a Something you write on = The assassin's chest is covered.

b Something you wear = The assassin wears a leopard skin.

c Something you eat = The assassin's chest is bare.

Now you should have all six clues!

THE AWESOME ANSWERS

Q1 They love it! Party scenes on tomb walls and songs on papyri show how much music and having a good time means to Egyptians. A small orchestra might contain harps, double oboes, flutes, lyres, lutes, tambourines, and rattles.

Q2 No. Sacred rattles (called sistrums) are often used in religious rites (*see page 9*), and flutes are played in the fields to help the reapers work (*see page 16*). Sometimes, musicians are often captured Syrians or Palestinians – 270 are captured by one pharaoh in a single campaign.

Cleopatra's Quest Answer:
You might see all of these things. To find out why, turn to page 29 and read the full answer.

The pharaoh's biggest worry is what happens to him after death. While he lives, he must treat his priests well so they carry out correctly the complicated rituals that will allow his soul to live forever. When he dies, embalmers will preserve his body – for by the time of the New Kingdom, they are experts at mummification. They will remove the internal organs and cover the body with crystals of a salt called natron, which stops the flesh from rotting.

Then the embalmers will pack his body with linen and resin and wrap it in linen strips. The corpse will be put in a coffin and the sacred rites carried out that will speed it on its way to the spirit world.

Q1 Where do mummies get their name from?

Q2 What happens in the afterlife?

Q3 Why don't Egyptians like going abroad?

MUMMY PUZZLE

The Egyptians love pets like dogs and monkeys. Some are so upset when a pet dies that they shave their own eyebrows! After the pets die, they are mummified so they will be with their owner in the afterlife. Can you spot four mummified animals in the main picture? Which of these do you think the Egyptians kept as pets?

MUMMY ANSWER
Mouse: Not really a pet. Cat: Yes, a popular pet. Giraffe: Queen Hatshepsut has a giraffe brought back for her zoo in 1490 B.C., but it isn't mummified. Crocodile: Not pets but they are mummified as sacred animals.

AWESOME ANSWERS

Q1 The word mummy comes from the Arabic word *mummiya*, meaning bitumen (tar), which medieval people mistakenly thought was the dark substance coating many mummies.

Q2 The Egyptians imagine that you enter a kingdom below the earth called Duat. On your way you will meet such horrors as lakes of fire and fire-spitting serpent demons. However, your coffin contains a set of scrolls known as the Book of the Dead, which is your passport through Duat. The scrolls contain all the spells needed to avoid the dangers.

PICKLE PUZZLE

The hardest job of the embalmers is to remove all the organs inside the body without making a horrible mess of the outside. Parts like the liver and lungs are taken out though a slit in the left side of the body, made with a special knife (*above*). These were then placed in special vessels called canopic jars (*right*). The heart was left in, so it could be "weighed" in the afterlife. The trickiest maneuver is taking out the brain. How do you think these needles are used to take it out (*left*)?

Cleopatra's Quest
Can you spot the water clock, thermos, doughnut, and crucifix? Which might you see in ancient Egypt?

The ultimate danger is the Hall of the Two Truths. Here your heart is "weighed" by Anubis. It is balanced against the feather of truth. If you pass the test, you reach a land like Egypt that is without worries or sadness. If you fail, your heart is eaten by a terrible monster, the Devourer.

Q3 The Egyptians are terrified that if they die abroad they won't get a proper burial, and so they will ruin their chances of reaching the spirit world. To them each person has three spirits: the *akh*, the *ka*, and the *ba*. Only the *akh* joins the spirit world – the *ba* and *ka* live on in the tomb.

PICKLE ANSWER
The brain is pulled through the nostril with the needles. Yuk!

Cleopatra's Quest Answer: You might see the water clock and doughnut. To find out why, turn to page 29.

THE PHARAOH'S TOMB

Q1 What is the Opening of the Mouth Ceremony?

THE AWESOME ANSWERS

Q1 In the Opening of the Mouth ceremony, a group of priests touch the features and hands of the mummy with ritual tools while reciting prayers. The ceremony allows the spirit of the pharaoh to eat, speak, and move in the afterlife.

Q2 Many of the tomb robbers are ancient Egyptians, often linked to the priests and craftsmen responsible for the tomb. For example, a coffin maker can be bribed to make a trap door in one end of the sarcophagus, so the heavy lids do not have to be removed. Also, court officials and guards are bribed to "look the other way." Finally, we know that tomb builders go on strike because they are unhappy about their wages. It is likely that they might turn to tomb robbing. The stealing continurs today.

On the side: **Q2 Who are the tomb robbers?**

Q3 Has anyone found a royal tomb that has not been robbed?

O n the day of the funeral, the pharaoh's mummy will be carried in procession to the mortuary temple for the Opening of the Mouth ceremony. After this, the mummy and coffin are dragged up to the entrance of the tomb. Priests will then carry the coffin through narrow passages to the burial chamber. The mummy will be placed in the sarcophagus (the large, stone, outer coffin), and the storerooms beside the burial chamber will be filled with the pharaoh's many possessions. Then the mourners will withdraw and the entrance to the tomb will be sealed.

The pharaoh must prepare (and pay) for all this before he dies. But, at the back of his mind, he knows that few tombs have escaped the robbers. For all his power, gody majesty, and his thousands of servants and soldiers, not even a pharaoh can be sure to outwit the tomb robbers.

A LUCKY ESCAPE

Most priests remained fiercely loyal to the pharaohs after their death. When some of them found out that the mummies were being stolen by important officials, they removed 30 other mummies and took them to a new hiding place.

Modern historians knew about these missing mummies, but it was only in the 1880s that archaeologist Emil Brugsch was led to a secret chamber. The 30 mummies (and some of their treasures) were safe at last. (They're now in the Cairo Museum).

🔲 **Cleopatra's Quest**
Can you spot the toy soldiers, bicycle, keys, razor, and Chinese writing? Which wouldn't you find in a pharaoh's tomb?

Q3 Yes. In 1922, archaeologist Howard Carter finds the tomb of Tutankhamen in the Valley of the Kings. A flight of steps leads to a passage filled with rubble, beyond which are rooms filled with fabulous treasures – and Tutankhamen is only a minor pharaoh.

🔲 *Cleopatra's Quest: You wouldn't find the bicycle or Chinese writing.* *To find out why, turn to page 29.*

A HOARD OF ANSWERS

CLEOPATRA'S QUEST

Pages 4–5

The Egyptians had *fishing nets* (which were first used in about 20,000 B.C.). They also had reed *canoes*, but did you notice that one of the canoes is a Native American design! No Egyptian boat was fast enough to pull a *water-skier*! The Egyptians had *pillows*, but preferred wooden headrests (*above right*) which let cool air circulate around their necks. Egyptians shaved their hair to be purer in spirit. Rich Egyptians wore *wigs* made of human hair (*left*), with vegetable fiber padding. They often placed a cone of wax on top of the wig. As the day wore on, the wax melted over the wig and a perfume was released.

Pages 6–7

Egyptian builders used *scaffolding* to build tall statues. There were no *slot machines* in New Kingdom Egypt, but in the first century A.D., the Greek inventor Heron designed a slot machine for use in Egyptian temples (*below right*). Worshipers placed a coin in the slot and received in return water to wash their hands and face before they entered the temple. Sacred *crocodiles* were kept for centuries in the temple of the crocodile god Sobek. *Sniffer dogs* were trained by the Egyptian police to hunt down criminals, just like today. Did you see the Nubian River Police on page 4? Temples were not designed for people to worship in, so there was no need for a *bell* to announce services. Ancient Egyptians didn't have the advanced *sundials* of the Romans, but they developed shadow clocks and water clocks (*see pages 24–25*) that gave a rough idea of time.

Pages 8–9

Musical *organs* were invented by an Egyptian, Ctesibus, in the 3rd century B.C. – too late for the New Kingdom. Bronze *mirrors* and *lipstick* were placed beside the statues of gods so they could look their best! The Egyptians had *shoes* made of leather, reeds, wood, and even sheet gold. Over 100 pairs of shoes were found in trendy King Tutankhamen's tomb!

Pages 10–11

As far as we know, there was no contact between ancient Egypt and China, so you wouldn't find *Chinese merchants* at the pharaoh's court. Ancient Egyptian *calendars* were divided into 365 days. Dates were written in red and black – the red days were the unlucky ones. Despite the heat, rich Egyptians were among the first people to wear *gloves*. New Kingdom pharaohs had zoo, but it would have been unlikely that *tigers* from Asia would have been on show. The Egyptians had long, brass *trumpets*, but without the valves found on the modern instruments.

Pages 12–13

Although it was not like a modern *sofa bed*, Tutankhamen did use a folding bed which he took with him on campaigns. *Baboons* were trained to collect ripe figs from trees for their owners! Electric *air conditioners* were not invented until the 20th century, but Roman Emperor Elagabalus (218–222 A.D.) had a mountain of snow erected in his villa in the summer to cool him down. Rich Egyptians were probably the first people to enjoy fishing as a sport. A drawing survives of a man with his *fishing rod* and line.

Pages 14–15

The first *typewriter* was only invented in 1867. As early as 4000 B.C. scribes were using pens made of reeds. But it wasn't until 500 B.C. that they had *quills* (pens from bird feathers). Scribes used a wooden palette as an *inkwell*. Craftsmen used a cord of fiber rather than a wooden *ruler*. Though cord stretches, their buildings were built with incredible accuracy.

Pages 16–17

Egyptian farmers used sickles to cut wheat, but the first *scythes* probably weren't around until Roman times. *Boomerang*-shaped throwsticks were used to hunt birds (*left*). The ancient Egyptians, obsessed with keeping their bodies clean, loved *underwear*!

Pages 18–19

The explosive *dynamite* was invented in 1867 by Alfred Nobel, a Swedish chemist who later founded the Nobel Prize. *Pneumatic drills* were first invented in the 20th century. Egyptian workmen ate *bag lunches* of bread, beer, and onions. Egyptian pharaohs operated a *pigeon post* system to send messages quickly

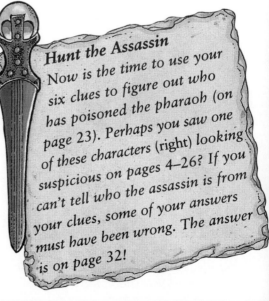

Hunt the Assassin
Now is the time to use your six clues to figure out who has poisoned the pharaoh (on page 23). Perhaps you saw one of these characters (right) looking suspicious on pages 4–26? If you can't tell who the assassin is from your clues, some of your answers must have been wrong. The answer is on page 32!

over long distances. *Knitting* was first invented in Egypt, but only in the 12th century A.D. Ancient Egyptian architects used a large version of a *level* to level out sites. A system of channels was dug in the ground and filled with water, since water always gives a level surface. This level was then marked and the channels drained. Any rock above the mark was removed and the channels filled with rubble to give a flat surface.

Pages 20–21

Egyptian soldiers rode ponies like *cavalry*, but they were only used as scouts. *Medals* for courage were awarded by the pharaoh. They were made of gold and shaped like a fly (*above right*). *Crossbows* were invented by the Chinese in the 4th century B.C. A *first-aid kit* was found in King Tutankhamen's tomb. The first war *elephants* were used in 4th-century B.C. India – too late for the Egyptian New Kingdom.

Pages 22–23

Egyptian women often had *tattoos*. Though without wind-up *mechanical mice*, Egyptian homes did have simple toys with moving jaws and other parts. They also loved *board games*, such as senet (*below left*). *Straws* were used to strain the lumps from Egyptian beer. The Egyptians did play *darts*, but threw long metal darts at a board on the floor.

Pages 24–25

The *crucifix* is a Christian symbol used from the 1st century A.D. onward. However, the Egyptian ankh ☥ does look similar. Bakers made at least 50 types of bread. These were sometimes shaped like animals, but were very different from what we call *doughnuts*. According to an inscription, in 1500 B.C. the Egyptian official Amenemhet invented the *water clock*. Water trickled through a hole in the bottom of the cup and time was measured by the drop in water (using marks on the sides). *Thermos* (or vacuum) *flasks,* used for keeping liquids hot or cold, were invented in 1892 by British chemist Sir James Dewar.

Pages 26–27

What we might call a *bicycle* wasn't invented until 1839. The Egyptians had bronze *razors* so huge they were probably used by professional barbers. The *toy soldiers* found in tombs weren't toys – they represented the servants the pharaoh might need in the spirit world. You wouldn't find *Chinese writing* in an Egyptian tomb – but Chinese mummies have been found dating from the 2nd century B.C. Egyptian *keys* worked using a clever system of strings (*left*).

TRUE OR FALSE

Page 5 *False* – They were built by peasant farmers during the flood season. **Page 7** *False* – There was no money! Instead of coins, Egyptians used rings of bronze that were carried on a larger ring (can you see any on page 11?). **Page 11** *True* – Priests were expected to be as pure as possible – they even shaved the hair off their bodies. **Page 18** *True* – The peppercorns were put in Ramesses's nose to preserve its hooked shape! **Page 20** *True* – Round stomachs were thought to be a sign of wealth. **Page 23** *True* – Royal tombs dating from about 2750 B.C. have been found with toilets. Can you see the toilet on page 30?

Play the Game
Once you have picked out the assassin, play the exciting Tomb Robbers' Game on pages 30–31.

Governor
Amenwau

Aunt
Tutu

Prince
Tuthmosis

Ay the
High Priest

Princess
Nefertari

Teye the
Servant

Nacht the
Scribe

Princess
Khnemhotpe

General
Panehsy

THE TOMB ROBBERS' GAME

1 BRIBING THE GUARDS

Travel through the Valley of Kings by bribing your way past the guards. However, you only have enough silver to pay four of them. Which guards are they?

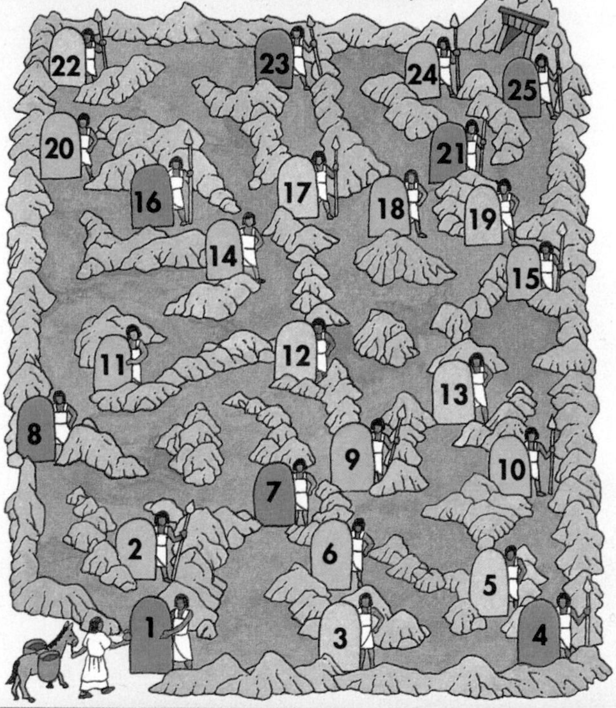

RULES OF THE GAME

You are after the pharaoh's treasure. First, find your way past the guards (puzzle 1), follow the right footprints (puzzle 2), and keep on track (puzzle 3). Once inside, get past the evil spirits by solving puzzles 4 to 6. These puzzles give you three hieroglyphs that combine to form a magic amulet! The answer is at the bottom of page 31.

5

6

7

7 THE FINAL CHALLENGE

Did you remember to write down the hieroglyphs given by your answers on puzzles 4 to 6. Now, combine the three hieroglyphs to create a magic amulet that will protect from the evil spirits that lurk within the final chamber.

A   B   C

D   E   F

30

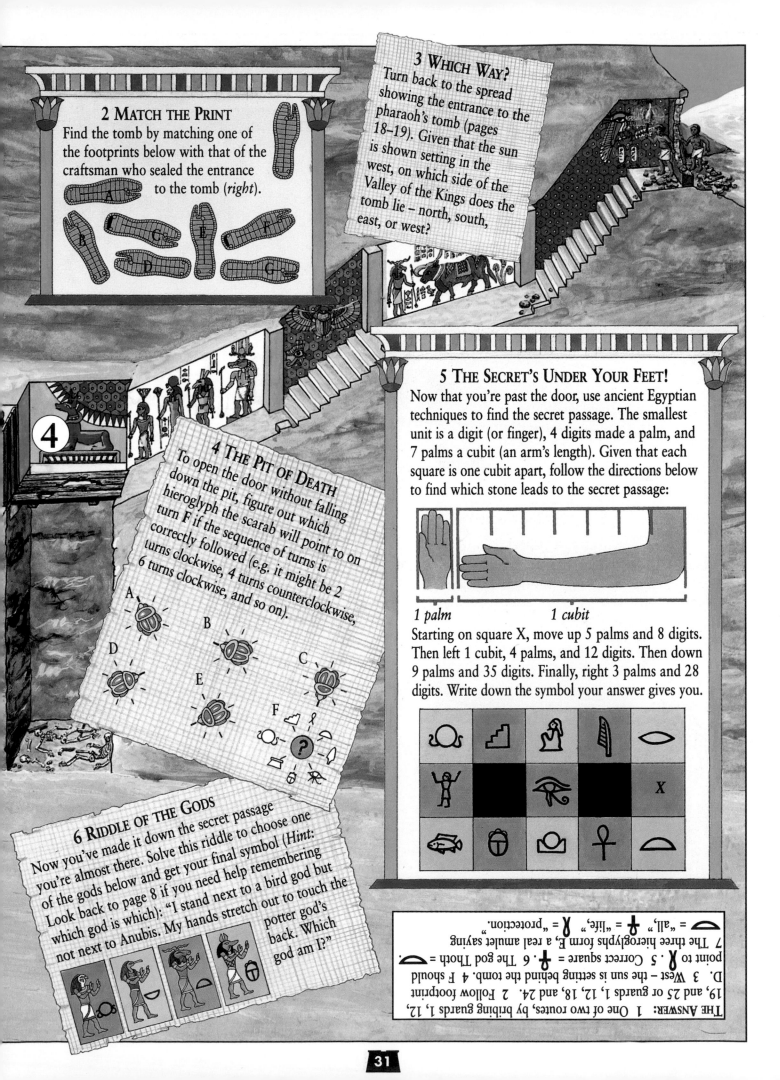

2 MATCH THE PRINT

Find the tomb by matching one of the footprints below with that of the craftsman who sealed the entrance to the tomb (*right*).

A B C D E F G

3 WHICH WAY?

Turn back to the spread showing the entrance to the pharaoh's tomb (pages 18–19). Given that the sun is shown setting in the west, on which side of the Valley of the Kings does the tomb lie – north, south, east, or west?

④

4 THE PIT OF DEATH

To open the door without falling down the pit, figure out which hieroglyph the scarab will point to on turn F if the sequence of turns is correctly followed (e.g. it might be 2 turns clockwise, 4 turns counterclockwise, 6 turns clockwise, and so on).

A
B
D
C
E
F ?

5 THE SECRET'S UNDER YOUR FEET!

Now that you're past the door, use ancient Egyptian techniques to find the secret passage. The smallest unit is a digit (or finger), 4 digits made a palm, and 7 palms a cubit (an arm's length). Given that each square is one cubit apart, follow the directions below to find which stone leads to the secret passage:

1 palm   1 cubit

Starting on square X, move up 5 palms and 8 digits. Then left 1 cubit, 4 palms, and 12 digits. Then down 9 palms and 35 digits. Finally, right 3 palms and 28 digits. Write down the symbol your answer gives you.

X

6 RIDDLE OF THE GODS

Now you've made it down the secret passage you're almost there. Solve this riddle to choose one of the gods below and get your final symbol (Hint: Look back to page 8 if you need help remembering which god is which): "I stand next to a bird god but not next to Anubis. My hands stretch out to touch the potter god's back. Which god am I?"

THE ANSWER: 1 One of two routes, by bribing guards 1, 12, 19, and 25 or guards 1, 12, 18, and 24. 2 Follow footprint D. 3 West – the sun is setting behind the tomb. 4 F should point to ʎ. 5 Correct square = ✝. 6 The god Thoth = ⌒. 7 The three hieroglyphs form E, a real amulet saying ⌒ = "all," ✝ = "life," ʎ = "protection."

31

INDEX

No Escape for the Assassin!
All along it was the wicked Princess Nefertari who was out to kill her brother and sieze the throne. Did you identify her? If you turn to page 23 you can see her watching the pharaoh as he chokes on her poisonous brew! Luckily the pharaoh recovered – so he won't be needing his tomb just yet!